Wilt Thou Be Made Whole?

(Breaking Free from the Victim Spirit)

Dr. C.B. Howard and Dr. Brenda Howard

ISBN 979-8-89526-135-4 (paperback)
ISBN 979-8-89526-136-1 (digital)

Copyright © 2024 by Dr. C.B. Howard and Dr. Brenda Howard

All rights reserved. No part of this publication may be reproduced, distributed, or transmitted in any form or by any means, including photocopying, recording, or other electronic or mechanical methods without the prior written permission of the publisher. For permission requests, solicit the publisher via the address below.

Christian Faith Publishing
832 Park Avenue
Meadville, PA 16335
www.christianfaithpublishing.com

The information contained in this book is intended to be educational. The authors are providing this information solely on the basis that the reader will be responsible for making their own assessments of the suitability of this information for their purposes.

Unless otherwise noted, the authors make no explicit guarantees as the accuracy of the information contained in this book may differ based on individual experiences and context.

Printed in the United States of America

Acknowledgments

"Now unto him that is able to do exceeding abundantly above all that we ask or think, according to the power that worketh in us."

—Ephesians 3:20

First, we give God the glory for allowing us to go through the many tests and trials that we can testify to the goodness and greatness of God and how He will bring us out of every situation from "victim to victor."

We thank our home church family, Tabernacle of Prayer Christian Fellowship, who experienced our struggles and still stand strong in faith. We also thank our family and those who encouraged us to put the knowledge in book form. Thank you, we love you very much.

Why This Book?

In many of today's churches and places of worship, Christians are taught to "name it and claim it" as a doctrine to make it through times of pain and suffering. One of the scriptures used to overcome difficult situations and challenging times is the Old Testament scripture:

> No weapon that is formed against thee shall prosper; and every tongue that shall rise against thee in judgment thou shalt condemn. This is the heritage of the servants of the Lord, and their righteousness is of me, saith the Lord. (Isaiah 54:17)

The passage above discusses the emotional and spiritual battles that many people face due to past experiences, such as negative relationships or mistreatment. It highlights the struggle of overcoming self-doubt and low self-esteem that can result from these past traumas. The authors emphasize the power of one's words in shaping one's experiences and suggest that addressing internal wounds is essential for experiencing true healing and deliverance.

This book serves as a valuable resource for individuals seeking healing from past hurts. The authors, drawing from personal experiences, share a message of hope and victory, encouraging readers to overcome their past and live a fulfilling life. As mother and son authors, we express courage and authenticity in sharing our journey through the book.

Ultimately, the book reinforces the idea that healing is an ongoing process and that the book can serve as a guide for individuals on their personal healing journeys.

Dr. Brenda Howard, DMin
C. B. Howard, DMin, EdD

Contents

Acknowledgments iii
Why This Book? v
Introduction ix
Who Is a Victim? 1
    Key characteristics of a victim mentality: 1
    The roots of victimhood 2
    The spiritual dimension 3
    Origins of the victim spirit 4
    Signs and symptoms of a victim mentality 7
The Cycle of Victimhood 9
    Bitterness and uncontrollable anger 9
    Pushing away help and support 10
    Finding faults in others 11
    Self-isolation and its consequences 12
    Breaking the cycle: a Christ-centered approach 15
The Power of Words 17
    Biblical perspective on the power of speech 17
    "Name it and claim it" doctrine: pros and cons 19
    Isaiah 54:17 in context 22
    Balancing faith declarations with inner healing 23
Generational Curses and Ancestral Sins 26
    Biblical understanding of generational influences 26
    Identifying generational patterns in your life 27
    Breaking free from ancestral sins 29

The Journey to Wholeness 32
   Acknowledging past traumas 33
   Confronting self-doubt and low self-esteem...............36
   Embracing vulnerability and authenticity................40
   Developing a healthy self-image rooted in Christ 41
Practical Steps for Healing...44
   Developing a strong support system 45
   Spiritual disciplines for inner healing 46
   Setting healthy boundaries 48
Overcoming Obstacles in the Healing Process 51
   Addressing ongoing negative relationships................52
   Navigating triggers and painful memories................54
   The role of perseverance and patience........................56
Living in Victory 58
   From victim to victor: changing your narrative 59
   Using your testimony to help others...........................61
   Continuing growth and maintaining wholeness.........65
Conclusion..69
   Final Words of Encouragement.................................69
   Call to action..70

Introduction

"Wilt thou be made whole?" These words, spoken by Jesus in John 5:6, echo through time, resonating with a power that transcends their original context. As we stand at the threshold of this book, this question serves as both an invitation and a challenge—one that we, as authors, have grappled with in our own lives and now extend to you, our readers.

The scene from John's Gospel is vivid and poignant. Jesus approaches a man who has been lying by the pool of Bethesda for thirty-eight years, paralyzed not just in body but seemingly in spirit as well. The man's condition is visible to all who pass by, a physical manifestation of the burdens he carries. Yet Jesus, in His infinite compassion, sees beyond the surface. He doesn't simply heal the man. He first asks a question that probes the depths of the human heart: "Do you want to get well?"

This question, simple on its face, unveils a profound truth about human nature. Sometimes, we become so accustomed to our pain, so familiar with our struggles, that the prospect of healing seems more daunting than the suffering itself. The paralyzed man's response is telling. Instead of a resounding "Yes!" he offers excuses and complaints about his lack of help, perhaps even a hint of self-pity. His words betray a spirit that has grown comfortable in its victimhood, wary of the responsibilities and self-reliance that wholeness would demand.

It is this spirit—what we term the "victim spirit"—that forms the central focus of our book. As authors, our journey to this point has been marked by personal encounters with this insidious force, both in our own lives and in the lives of countless individuals we've encountered in our ministries and communities. We've witnessed firsthand the devastating effects of this mindset and how it can take root in the fertile soil of rejection, trauma, and generational curses, growing into a strangling vine that chokes out hope, joy, and the abundant life Christ promises.

Our purpose in writing this book is born from a deep-seated desire to see individuals break free from the chains of victimhood and step into the fullness of their God-given potential. We believe that the epidemic of the victim spirit is one of the most pressing issues facing the body of Christ today. It manifests in myriad ways—in the bitter and angry person who pushes away help, in the individual constantly finding fault with others to keep them at a distance, and in the believer who can quote scripture about victory but remains trapped in cycles of defeat.

The concept of the victim spirit goes beyond mere negative thinking or low self-esteem. It is a complex interplay of psychological, spiritual, and often generational factors that create a perfect storm of perpetual victimhood. This spirit acts as a beacon, signaling vulnerability to potential perpetrators and creating a heightened sense of vigilance that anticipates and even subconsciously invites further harm. It's a self-fulfilling prophecy that keeps individuals trapped in cycles of abuse, control, and self-sabotage.

But there is hope—profound, life-changing hope!

Through the pages of this book, we will embark on a journey of understanding, healing, and transformation. We'll explore the roots of the victim spirit, delving into topics such as pre-birth rejection, childhood trauma, and the controversial but biblical concept of generational curses. We'll examine the cycle of victimhood, shining a light on the patterns of behavior that keep individuals trapped in this destructive mindset.

Central to our discussion will be the power of words. The Bible tells us that death and life are in the power of the tongue (Proverbs 18:21), and we'll unpack this truth, examining how our speech can either reinforce our victimhood or pave the way for our liberation. We'll take a balanced look at teachings like the "name it and claim it" doctrine, seeking to understand how faith declarations can be a powerful tool for change when coupled with genuine inner healing.

WILT THOU BE MADE WHOLE?

As we progress, we'll confront the reality of generational curses and ancestral sins. This isn't about assigning blame or wallowing in past hurts; it's about identifying patterns, understanding their origins, and learning how to break free from cycles that may have plagued our families for generations. We'll discover the crucial role of forgiveness in this process, not as a mere platitude but as a powerful act of self-liberation.

The journey to wholeness is not a simple one, and we won't pretend otherwise. We'll address the very real challenges of confronting past traumas, battling self-doubt and low self-esteem, and learning to embrace vulnerability and authenticity. Together, we'll explore practical steps for healing, from seeking professional help and building strong support systems to engaging in spiritual disciplines that foster inner healing.

Throughout this book, we'll return time and again to the foundational truth of our identity in Christ. For it is only when we truly grasp who we are in Him—beloved, chosen, and empowered—that we can fully break free from the victim spirit and step into the role of victor.

Our journey together will not end with personal healing. We believe that as you experience transformation, you'll be equipped to help others break free from their cycles of victimhood. Your testimony will become a powerful tool for bringing hope and healing to your family, your community, and beyond.

As we close this introduction, we want to acknowledge that the path ahead may not be easy. There will likely be moments of discomfort as we confront hard truths and deep-seated patterns. But we assure you, the freedom that awaits on the other side is worth every step of the journey.

So we return to that piercing question Jesus asked by the pool of Bethesda: "Wilt thou be made whole?" It's a question that demands a response, not just in words, but in action. It's an invitation to step out of the familiar, albeit painful, patterns of victimhood and into the fullness of life that God intends for you.

As you turn these pages, our prayer is that you'll freshly encounter the living God. If you allow His love to penetrate the deepest wounds of your heart, you'll find the courage to confront the victim's spirit head-on, declaring with conviction, "I refuse to be victimized again!"

Are you ready to be made whole? Are you prepared to break free from generational curses, to rewrite your narrative from victim to victor, to reclaim your God-given freedom not just for yourself but for generations to come?

If your answer is yes, then let's begin this transformative journey together. The path to wholeness awaits.

Who Is a Victim?

But they that wait upon the Lord shall renew their strength; they shall mount up with wings as eagles; they shall run, and not be weary; they shall walk and not faint.

—Isaiah 40:31

To truly understand the journey from victimhood to victory, we must first grasp what it means to be a victim in the context of the "victim spirit." This understanding is crucial for recognizing patterns in our own lives and taking steps toward healing and wholeness.

Webster's dictionary defines a victim as "a living being offered as a sacrifice; an individual injured or killed by disease or argument, or a person that has been cheated, fooled, or injured." However, in the context of this book and the concept of the "victim spirit," we're looking at a more complex and nuanced definition that goes beyond a single incident of victimization.

A victim we're exploring, in a sense, is someone who has internalized a sense of powerlessness and helplessness that pervades multiple areas of their life. This internalization often stems from genuine experiences of trauma, abuse, or persistent negative circumstances, but it can also be the result of perceived slights or a distorted worldview.

Key characteristics of a victim mentality:

1. Persistent feelings of powerlessness: victims often feel that they have little to no control over their lives or circumstances.

2. Blame-shifting: rather than taking responsibility for their actions or circumstances, victims tend to blame others or external factors for their problems.
3. Self-pity: victims often indulge in self-pity, viewing themselves as the unfortunate targets of life's cruelties.
4. Negative self-image: many victims struggle with low self-esteem and a negative self-image.
5. Resistance to change: despite expressing a desire for things to be different, victims often resist genuine opportunities for change.
6. Difficulty in relationships: victims may struggle to maintain healthy relationships due to their tendency to blame others or seek constant validation.
7. Passive-aggressive behavior: unable to express their needs or frustrations directly, victims may resort to passive-aggressive tactics.

It's important to note that being a victim of a crime or traumatic event does not automatically equate to having a victim mentality. Many individuals who have experienced genuine victimization are able to process their experiences in healthy ways and move forward without internalizing a victim identity. The difference lies in how one responds to and interprets their experiences over time.

The roots of victimhood

Understanding how someone becomes entrenched in a victim mentality is crucial for breaking free from it. Several factors can contribute to the development of a victim spirit:

1. Childhood experiences: early experiences of neglect, abuse, or persistent disappointment can lay the groundwork for a victim mentality. Children who grow up in environments where their needs are consistently unmet may develop a sense of helplessness that carries into adulthood.

2. Generational patterns: as mentioned in our outline, generational curses or patterns of behavior can play a significant role. Children who grow up observing their parents or grandparents exhibit victim behaviors may unconsciously adopt these same patterns.
3. Traumatic events: significant traumas, especially when unprocessed or inadequately addressed, can lead to a persistent sense of victimhood. This is particularly true when the trauma is repeated or prolonged.
4. Societal and cultural factors: certain societal or cultural environments may inadvertently reinforce victim mentalities, particularly in marginalized or oppressed communities. While acknowledging real systemic issues, it's important to distinguish between fighting for justice and becoming trapped in a victim identity.
5. Spiritual warfare: from a Christian perspective, we must also consider the role of spiritual forces. The enemy seeks to keep God's children bound in lies and false identities, and the victim spirit can be a powerful tool in this regard.

The spiritual dimension

As Christians, it's crucial to understand the spiritual implications of the victim mentality. The Bible tells us that we are more than conquerors through Christ (Romans 8:37) and that "God has not given us a spirit of fear but of power, love, and a sound mind" (2 Timothy 1:7). A victim mentality stands in direct opposition to these truths.

The victim spirit can be seen as a stronghold that keeps believers from fully embracing their identity in Christ and walking in the freedom and authority He has given them. It can hinder spiritual growth, limit effective ministry, and create barriers in one's relationship with God and others.

Moreover, remaining in a victim mentality can be a form of idolatry, placing one's wounds and past experiences at the center of one's identity rather than one's relationship with Christ. It can lead to a distorted view of God, seeing Him as distant, uncaring, or even as the source of one's pain rather than the source of healing and redemption.

Origins of the victim spirit

Understanding the roots of the victim spirit is crucial for addressing it effectively. While each individual's journey is unique, there are common origins that we often see:

1. Pre-birth rejection

The concept of pre-birth rejection may seem strange at first, but it's a reality that many face. This can occur in several ways:

- Unwanted pregnancies: when a child is conceived in circumstances where they are not wanted or welcomed, it can create a spiritual and emotional wound even before birth.
- Attempted abortions: if there were attempts or considerations of abortion during the pregnancy, this could create a deep-seated sense of rejection in the child.
- Parental stress or trauma: if the mother experiences significant stress, trauma, or negative emotions during pregnancy, this can impact the developing child's emotional and spiritual formation.
- Generational curses: as we'll discuss later, spiritual influences from previous generations can begin to affect a child even in the womb.

The impact of pre-birth rejection can be profound, creating a foundation of insecurity and a sense of being unwanted that can persist throughout life if not addressed.

2. Childhood Trauma

Childhood experiences play a crucial role in shaping our worldview and emotional responses. Traumatic experiences during these formative years can significantly contribute to the development of a victim spirit:

- Physical or sexual abuse: these severe forms of trauma can shatter a child's sense of safety and self-worth, laying the groundwork for a victim mentality.
- Emotional abuse or neglect: consistent criticism, belittling, or emotional unavailability from caregivers can instill a deep sense of unworthiness and helplessness.
- Witnessing domestic violence: even if not directly targeted, children who witness violence in the home can develop a victim mentality as a coping mechanism.
- Bullying: persistent bullying at school or in other social settings can reinforce feelings of powerlessness and isolation.
- Loss or abandonment: the death of a parent, divorce, or other forms of abandonment can create deep-seated fears and insecurities.
- Chronic illness or disability: children dealing with ongoing health issues may develop a victim mentality as a way of coping with their limitations and differences.

3. Generational curses

The concept of generational curses is rooted in biblical understanding, as seen in Exodus 20:5:

> You shall not bow down to them or serve them, for I the Lord your God am a jealous God, visiting the iniquity of the fathers on the children to the third and the fourth generation of those who hate me.

Generational curses are passed down through the years in patterns that seem to happen over and over. It's seen in parents and grandparents, and if you search further, you find some of the same patterns and behaviors in other generations. Have you asked yourself why it is that my parents and grandparents experienced the same struggles that their ancestors experienced? And I notice them manifesting in myself and my children. If you are saved, you can break the generational curse and see your children and grandchildren experience a new and better life. It's time to break those old mindsets and move to establish new mindsets that get results. When the patterns don't fit anymore, you need to get a new pattern. So often, people see the patterns but don't know what to do to stop them. People stay in these patterns of behavior for many generations because it becomes the norm. They realize that they are not prospering but are stuck and, after a while, become content with that lifestyle. Often, many are stuck listening to family members who can't see their way out and don't want you to come out. It amazes me how family members say they want to come out but are not willing to do the work and don't want you to get out of the cycle. Generational curses manifest in the spirit of poverty, having children out of wedlock, and staying in mediocre jobs because you fear your family will criticize you for doing something different. Don't be fearful. "God did not give us the spirit of fear but of love, power, and a sound mind" (1 Timothy 3:7). Personally, I saw my family members from generation to generation get on welfare, and I made a decision not to allow myself to follow that pattern. Thanks be to God that making that decision and not reverting back to the old patterns has allowed not only my immediate family members but others in the family to seek to do better.

- Inherited trauma: unresolved trauma from previous generations can be passed down through family systems and behaviors.
- Learned behaviors: children often model the coping mechanisms and worldviews of their parents, perpetuating victim mentalities across generations.
- Spiritual bondage: from a spiritual perspective, unaddressed sin or spiritual agreements made by ancestors can have lingering effects on subsequent generations.
- Cultural or societal oppression: historical traumas experienced by certain ethnic or cultural groups can create a

WILT THOU BE MADE WHOLE?

collective victim mentality that is passed down through generations.

Understanding these generational influences is crucial for breaking the cycle and stepping into freedom.

Signs and symptoms of a victim mentality

Recognizing the signs and symptoms of a victim mentality is the first step toward overcoming it. Here are some key indicators:

1. Constant complaining: a tendency to focus on and vocalize everything wrong in one's life.
2. Difficulty accepting responsibility: consistently blaming others or circumstances for one's problems or failures.
3. Feeling powerless: a pervasive sense that one has no control over one's life or circumstances.
4. Negative self-talk: internal dialogue that reinforces feelings of worthlessness or hopelessness.
5. Attention-seeking behavior: using one's misfortunes to garner sympathy or attention from others.
6. Difficulty making decisions: Paralysis in decision-making due to fear of making the wrong choice.
7. Chronic pessimism: always expecting the worst and unable to see positive possibilities.
8. Resistance to change: clinging to familiar patterns even when they're harmful, out of fear or comfort with the known.
9. Envy and resentment: feeling that others have it better and harboring bitterness about perceived injustices.
10. Self-sabotage: unconsciously creating situations that reinforce the victim narrative.
11. Difficulty accepting compliments: deflecting praise or positive feedback, unable to internalize positive messages.
12. Persistent anger or irritability: often stemming from a sense of injustice or powerlessness.

13. Isolation: withdrawing from relationships or avoiding new connections out of fear or a belief that no one understands.
14. Physical symptoms: chronic stress from maintaining a victim mentality can manifest in physical ailments like headaches, digestive issues, or fatigue.
15. Spiritual disconnection: difficulty trusting God or feeling His presence, often accompanied by questions like "Why me?" or "How could God allow this?"

Understanding the victim's spirit, its origins, and its manifestations is a crucial step in the journey toward healing and freedom. By recognizing these patterns in our lives, we open the door to transformation. In the chapters that follow, we will explore practical strategies and spiritual truths that will help us break free from the victim spirit and step into the victorious life God intends for us.

Remember, identifying with aspects of the victim's spirit is not a cause for shame or despair. Rather, it's an opportunity for growth, healing, and renewed dependence on God's grace and power. As we continue this journey, hold fast to the truth of 2 Corinthians 5:17: "Therefore, if anyone is in Christ, the new creation has come: The old has gone, the new is here!"

The Cycle of Victimhood

The victim spirit, once entrenched, often manifests as a self-perpetuating cycle that can be challenging to break. This cycle of victimhood reinforces negative patterns of thought and behavior, creating a downward spiral that impacts every aspect of an individual's life. Therefore, we need to explore the key components of this cycle: bitterness and uncontrollable anger, pushing away help and support, finding faults in others, and self-isolation. Understanding these elements and their interconnectedness is crucial for breaking free from the victim mentality and stepping into a life of victory and purpose.

Bitterness and uncontrollable anger

At the core of the victimhood cycle often lies a deep well of bitterness and anger. These emotions, while natural responses to hurt and injustice, can become toxic when left unaddressed.

1. The root of bitterness: bitterness typically stems from unresolved hurt, disappointment, or perceived injustice. For those trapped in a victim mentality, these feelings can become all-consuming. Hebrews 12:15 warns us about this danger: "See to it that no one falls short of the grace of God and that no bitter root grows up to cause trouble and defile many."

   Bitterness acts like a poison, contaminating not just the individual's thoughts and actions but also their relationships and spiritual life. It creates a lens through which all experiences are filtered, reinforcing the belief that life is unfair and that one is perpetually victimized.

DR. C.B. HOWARD AND DR. BRENDA HOWARD

2. The manifestation of uncontrollable anger: as bitterness festers, it often erupts as uncontrollable anger. This anger may be:

    *   Disproportionate: small triggers lead to explosive reactions.
    *   Misdirected: anger is vented on innocent parties or unrelated situations.
    *   Chronic: a constant state of irritability and rage becomes the norm.
    *   Self-destructive: anger is turned inward, leading to self-harm or self-sabotage.

    Ephesians 4:26–27 advises, "In your anger do not sin: Do not let the sun go down while you are still angry, and do not give the devil a foothold." Uncontrolled anger not only damages relationships but also provides an entry point for further spiritual bondage.

3. The cycle of bitterness and anger: Bitterness fuels anger, and expressions of anger often lead to further isolation or conflict, which in turn deepens the sense of victimization and bitterness. This creates a self-reinforcing cycle that's difficult to break without intentional intervention and healing.

Pushing away help and support

One of the most paradoxical aspects of the victimhood cycle is the tendency to push away the very help and support that could facilitate healing and growth.

1. Fear of vulnerability: individuals trapped in a victim mentality often develop a fear of being hurt again. This fear can manifest as a reluctance to open up or trust others, even when genuine help is offered. The vulnerability required to accept support feels too risky.

WILT THOU BE MADE WHOLE?

2. Maintaining the victim identity: subconsciously, accepting help might threaten the victim identity that has become a core part of one's self-concept. There can be a perverse comfort in remaining in the familiar role of the victim, even if it's painful.

3. Mistrust of others' motives: past experiences of betrayal or disappointment can lead to a generalized mistrust of others' intentions. Offers of help may be viewed with suspicion or as having hidden agendas.

4. Self-sabotage: even when help is initially accepted, there may be a tendency to sabotage the support through non-compliance, conflict, or sudden withdrawal. This behavior reinforces the belief that "nothing ever works out" for the victim.

5. The illusion of self-sufficiency: paradoxically, some individuals in the victimhood cycle may push away help in an attempt to prove their self-sufficiency or to avoid feeling indebted to others.

Proverbs 12:15 reminds us, "The way of fools seems right to them, but the wise listen to advice." Pushing away help not only prevents healing but also reinforces isolation and the belief that one must face life's challenges alone.

Finding faults in others

A key characteristic of the victimhood cycle is the tendency to constantly find faults in others. This behavior serves several psychological functions within the cycle:

1. Deflection of responsibility: by focusing on the faults of others, individuals avoid confronting their own issues or taking responsibility for their circumstances. It's easier to blame others than to engage in the difficult work of self-reflection and change.

2. Justification of victimhood: identifying faults in others provides justification for one's victim status. It reinforces

the belief that "everyone is against me" or that the world is inherently unfair.

3. Projection of inner turmoil: often, the faults we most readily see in others are reflections of our own inner struggles. This projection allows individuals to externalize their internal conflicts.

4. Maintaining a sense of superiority: paradoxically, constantly criticizing others can provide a false sense of moral or intellectual superiority, temporarily boosting low self-esteem.

5. Creating distance: finding faults in others creates emotional distance, protecting the individual from the vulnerability of close relationships.

Matthew 7:3–5 speaks directly to this tendency: "Why do you look at the speck of sawdust in your brother's eye and pay no attention to the plank in your own eye? How can you say to your brother, 'Let me take the speck out of your eye,' when all the time there is a plank in your own eye? You hypocrite, first take the plank out of your own eye, and then you will see clearly to remove the speck from your brother's eye."

This habit of faultfinding not only damages relationships but also prevents personal growth and healing. It keeps the individual focused outward, avoiding the inward reflection necessary for breaking the cycle of victimhood.

Self-isolation and its consequences

The culmination of bitterness, pushing away help, and finding faults in others often leads to self-isolation. This isolation, while initially a defense mechanism, carries severe consequences that further entrench the victimhood cycle.

1. The path to isolation

   • Withdrawal from relationships: gradually pulling away from friends, family, and social activities.

- Avoidance of new connections: reluctance to form new relationships or engage in new social situations.
- Creating physical barriers: sometimes manifesting as actual physical isolation, spending excessive time alone.
- Emotional disconnection: even when physically present, maintaining an emotional distance from others.

2. Perceived benefits of isolation

- Protection from hurt: isolation can feel like a safe haven from potential rejection or disappointment.
- Control: being alone provides a sense of control over one's environment and interactions.
- Avoidance of accountability: isolation removes the challenge of having one's victim narrative questioned or confronted.

3. Consequences of self-isolation

Emotional consequences

- Deepening depression: lack of social interaction and support can exacerbate depressive tendencies.
- Increased anxiety: isolation often leads to increased worry and fear about the outside world.
- Reinforced negative self-Image: without positive external input, negative self-perceptions go unchallenged.

Mental consequences

- Cognitive distortions: isolation allows irrational thoughts and beliefs to grow unchecked.
- Decreased problem-solving skills: lack of diverse interactions reduces exposure to different perspectives and problem-solving approaches.

- Rumination: excessive time alone can lead to unhealthy dwelling on negative thoughts and experiences.

Physical consequences

- Weakened immune system: chronic isolation has been linked to decreased immune function.
- Increased health risks: studies have shown that isolation increases risks for various health issues, including heart disease and stroke.
- Neglect of self-care: isolation often correlates with decreased motivation for proper nutrition, exercise, and hygiene.

Spiritual consequences

- Disconnection from the community: isolation removes the individual from the support and accountability of a faith community.
- Vulnerability to spiritual attack: Ecclesiastes 4:12 warns, "Though one may be overpowered, two can defend themselves. A cord of three strands is not quickly broken." Isolation leaves one more vulnerable to spiritual struggles.
- Distorted view of God: without the balance of community, one's perception of God can become skewed, often viewing Him through the lens of victimhood.

Relational consequences:

- Atrophied social skills: Extended isolation can lead to a decreased ability to navigate social interactions effectively.
- Missed opportunities: isolation results in missed chances for personal growth, career advancement, and meaningful relationships.
- Burden on existing relationships: The few relationships that remain often become strained under the weight of the individual's needs and negative outlook.

WILT THOU BE MADE WHOLE?

Breaking the cycle: a Christ-centered approach

Recognizing the destructive nature of the victimhood cycle is the first step toward breaking free from it. As believers, we have the power of Christ within us to overcome these patterns. Here are some biblically-based steps toward breaking the cycle of victimhood:

1. Acknowledge the pattern through prayerful self-examination (Psalm 139:23): "Search me, O God, and know my heart; test me and know my anxious thoughts." Invite the Holy Spirit to reveal these patterns in your life. Remember, conviction is not condemnation; it's an opportunity for growth in Christ.

2. Seek godly counsel (Proverbs 11:14): "Where there is no guidance, a people falls, but in an abundance of counselors there is safety." Seek wisdom from mature believers, pastoral counseling, or Christian therapists who can provide biblically-based strategies for addressing the root causes of the victimhood cycle.

3. Renew your mind with God's Word (Romans 12:2): "Do not conform to the pattern of this world, but be transformed by the renewing of your mind." Actively replace negative thought patterns with God's truth. Memorize and meditate on Scripture that affirms your identity in Christ and God's love for you.

4. Practice Biblical Gratitude (1 Thessalonians 5:18): "Give thanks in all circumstances; for this is God's will for you in Christ Jesus." Cultivate a heart of thankfulness, focusing on God's blessings and faithfulness even in difficult circumstances.

5. Take steps toward biblical community (Hebrews 10:24–25): "And let us consider how we may spur one another on toward love and good deeds, not giving up meeting together." Gradually rebuild connections within the body of Christ, starting with safe, supportive relationships in your church or small group.

6. Embrace God's forgiveness and extend it to others (Colossians 3:13): "Bear with each other and forgive one another if any of you has a grievance against someone. Forgive as the Lord forgave you." Accept God's forgiveness for yourself and, through His strength, extend forgiveness to others. This is crucial for breaking free from bitterness and anger.

7. Engage in the Christian community (Proverbs 27:17): "Iron sharpens iron, and one man sharpens another." Immerse yourself in a Bible-believing church community that can provide encouragement, accountability, and a Christ-centered perspective on your challenges.

8. Put on the full armor of God (Ephesians 6:11): "Put on the full armor of God, so that you can take your stand against the devil's schemes." Recognize that breaking free from the victimhood cycle is a spiritual battle. Daily, clothe yourself in God's armor through prayer and faith.

9. Find your identity in Christ (2 Corinthians 5:17): "Therefore, if anyone is in Christ, the new creation has come: The old has gone, the new is here!" Constantly remind yourself of who you are in Christ—beloved, redeemed, and empowered by the Holy Spirit.

10. Submit to God's healing process (Psalm 147:3): "He heals the brokenhearted and binds up their wounds." Trust in God's desire and ability to heal you. Submit to his process, which may involve confronting painful truths but always leads to freedom and wholeness.

Remember, breaking free from the victimhood cycle is not just about escaping negative patterns; it's about stepping into the abundant life that Christ promises. As Jesus said, "The thief comes only to steal and kill and destroy; I have come that they may have life, and have it to the full." Through Christ, you have the power to break this cycle and walk in the freedom and victory He has secured for you.

The Power of Words

In the journey from victimhood to wholeness, there is a powerful tool that can either propel us forward or hold us back: our words. This chapter explores the profound impact of speech in our lives, rooted deeply in biblical wisdom and practical experience. From the creation account in Genesis to the teachings of Jesus and the apostles, Scripture consistently emphasizes the weight our words carry in shaping our reality and influencing those around us.

Let's examine the biblical perspective on the power of speech, critically assess the "Name it and Claim it" doctrine, and unpack the rich context of Isaiah 54:17. Through this exploration, you'll discover how to align your speech with God's truth, confront negative self-talk, and use your words as a force for positive change in your life.

Remember, the words you speak are not just sounds; they are seeds planted in the garden of your life. Let's learn how to cultivate speech that nurtures growth, healing, and transformation.

Biblical perspective on the power of speech

Have you ever stopped to think about the words you use every day? The casual conversations, the inner dialogues, the whispered prayers? In our fast-paced world, it's easy to forget just how powerful our words can be. But the Bible reminds us, time and time again, that our speech carries more weight than we often realize.

Let's take a journey back to the very beginning. In Genesis 1, we see God speaking the world into existence. "Let there be light," he says, and suddenly, darkness gives way to brilliant illumination. With each day of creation, God's words shape reality, bringing forth land

and sea, plants and animals, and finally, humankind. It's a stunning display of the creative power of words, setting the stage for how we understand language throughout the rest of Scripture.

Now imagine sitting with King Solomon, known for his wisdom, as he shares a profound truth. In Proverbs 18:21, he tells us, "Death and life are in the power of the tongue, and those who love it will eat its fruits." It's a statement that might make us pause and reflect. Our words, Solomon says, have the power to bring either life or death. They can be a source of blessing or curse, not just for others but for ourselves as well.

Think about it: how often have your own words shaped your reality? Maybe you've talked yourself out of trying something new, reinforcing fears and limitations. Or perhaps you've spoken words of encouragement to a friend, helping them find strength they didn't know they had. Our speech doesn't just describe our world; it helps create it.

Fast forward to the New Testament, where James, the brother of Jesus, has some particularly pointed things to say about our speech. In James 3:3–5, he paints a vivid picture:

> When we put bits into the mouths of horses to make them obey us, we can turn the whole animal. Or take ships as an example. Although they are so large and are driven by strong winds, they are steered by a very small rudder wherever the pilot wants to go. Likewise, the tongue is a small part of the body, but it makes great boasts.

Can you visualize it? A massive ship, tossed by wind and waves yet guided by a tiny rudder. It's a powerful metaphor for how our words, seemingly small and insignificant, can steer the entire course of our lives. The off-hand comment that sparks a lifelong friendship, the thoughtless remark that damages a relationship, the words of faith spoken in a moment of doubt—all these can change our direction in profound ways.

WILT THOU BE MADE WHOLE?

But it's not just James who emphasizes the importance of our speech. Jesus himself, in Matthew 12:36–37, offers a sobering reminder: "But I tell you that everyone will have to give account on the day of judgment for every empty word they have spoken. For by your words you will be acquitted, and by your words you will be condemned."

Let that sink in for a moment. Every word—even the ones we consider throwaway comments or idle chatter—carries weight in God's eyes. It's a responsibility that might feel heavy at first, but it's also an invitation to intentionality. What if we approached each conversation, each prayer, and each self-talk moment with the awareness that our words matter deeply?

This awareness becomes crucial! We need to pay attention to the narratives we're crafting with our words. Are we speaking life into our situations, or are we reinforcing patterns of negativity and defeat? Are our words aligning with God's truth about who we are, or are they echoing the lies we've believed for too long?

Take a moment to reflect on your own speech patterns. Think about the last conversation you had or the thoughts that have been running through your mind today. Are they words of hope, of possibility, of faith? Or do they lean towards criticism, doubt, or self-defeat?

Remember, changing our speech isn't about denying reality or plastering on fake positivity. It's about aligning our words with God's truth, even when, especially when, our circumstances seem to contradict it. It's about speaking life, hope, and faith, not because everything is perfect, but because we serve a God who can bring beauty from ashes and joy from mourning.

"Name it and claim it" doctrine: pros and cons

The "Name it and claim it" doctrine, rooted in the Word of Faith movement, has become a significant and controversial aspect of contemporary Christian thought. This teaching emphasizes the power of positive confession and faith-filled declarations to manifest desired outcomes in a believer's life. While it has gained a con-

19

siderable following, it has also faced substantial criticism within the broader Christian community.

Pros:

1. Encourages active faith: this doctrine challenges believers to move beyond passive belief to active faith. It encourages Christians to boldly approach God with their needs and desires, as seen in Hebrews 4:16: "Let us then approach God's throne of grace with confidence, so that we may receive mercy and find grace to help us in our time of need." This active engagement with faith can lead to a more dynamic and personal relationship with God.

2. Emphasizes the power of words: the focus on the power of speech aligns with biblical principles. Proverbs 18:21 states, "The tongue has the power of life and death, and those who love it will eat its fruit." This doctrine reminds believers of the importance of speaking positive and faith-filled words, which can have a transformative effect on one's mindset and actions.

3. Promotes positive thinking: by encouraging believers to focus on God's promises rather than current circumstances, this teaching can foster resilience and hope. It aligns with Paul's exhortation in Philippians 4:8 to think about "*Whatever is true, whatever is noble, whatever is right, whatever is pure, whatever is lovely, whatever is admirable.*" This positive focus can be particularly beneficial for those struggling with depression, anxiety, or difficult life circumstances.

4. Cultivates expectancy: the doctrine fosters an expectant attitude toward God's intervention in one's life. This can lead to increased prayer, heightened spiritual awareness, and a greater openness to recognizing God's work in daily life.

WILT THOU BE MADE WHOLE?

Cons:

1. Oversimplification of faith: while the doctrine encourages bold faith, it can oversimplify the complex nature of spiritual growth and life's challenges. It may not adequately address the reality of suffering in the Christian life, as exemplified by Paul's "thorn in the flesh" (2 Corinthians 12:7–10). This oversimplification can lead to disillusionment when prayers aren't answered as expected.

2. Misinterpretation and proof-texting: proponents of this doctrine sometimes isolate verses to support their claims without considering the broader context of scripture. For example, John 14:14 ("You may ask me for anything in my name, and I will do it") is often cited without considering the context of aligning one's will with God's purposes. This approach can lead to a distorted understanding of biblical principles.

3. Potential for spiritual blame and guilt: when desired outcomes don't materialize, this teaching can lead to blaming the individual for lack of faith. This can create a cycle of guilt and spiritual performance anxiety, potentially damaging one's relationship with God. It may also trivialize complex issues like physical illness or financial hardship by suggesting they are simply the result of insufficient faith.

4. Overemphasis on material prosperity: while God does bless His people, an overemphasis on material prosperity can distort the Christian message. It may lead to a transactional view of faith, where God is seen as a means to personal gain rather than the ultimate goal of devotion. This perspective can conflict with biblical teachings on contentment (Philippians 4:11–13) and the value of spiritual riches over material wealth (Matthew 6:19–21).

5. Neglect of God's Sovereignty: The doctrine can sometimes downplay God's sovereignty in favor of human faith declarations. This may lead to a view where humans appear to control God through their words rather than submitting

to His will. It's important to balance faith with an understanding of God's ultimate authority and wisdom.

6. Potential for spiritual pride: those who seem to experience success with this approach may develop spiritual pride, viewing their prosperity as a sign of superior faith. This attitude can lead to judgment of others who are struggling, contradicting biblical teachings on humility and compassion.

7. Neglect of character development: by focusing heavily on external blessings, this teaching may underemphasize the importance of character development, spiritual fruit, and Christ-like transformation, which are central to biblical Christianity.

While the "name it and claim it" doctrine highlights important aspects of faith, such as bold prayer and positive confession, it requires careful examination and balance. Christians should be encouraged to approach God with confidence and speak faith-filled words, but also to embrace the full counsel of Scripture, including teachings on suffering, God's sovereignty, and the primacy of spiritual growth over material gain. A mature faith recognizes both the power of words and the complexity of walking with God in a fallen world.

Isaiah 54:17 in context

Isaiah 54:17 is a verse often cited in discussions about the power of words and spiritual warfare: "'*No weapon forged against you will prevail, and you will refute every tongue that accuses you. This is the heritage of the servants of the Lord, and this is their vindication from me,*' declares the Lord."

To fully understand this verse, we need to examine its context. Isaiah 54 is a prophecy of hope and restoration for Israel after a period of exile and suffering. God is promising to restore his people and protect them from their enemies.

WILT THOU BE MADE WHOLE?

Key points to consider:

1. God's sovereignty: the protection and vindication come from God, not from the power of our words alone.
2. Covenant relationship: this promise is given to "the servants of the Lord," emphasizing the importance of a right relationship with God.
3. Refuting accusations: while God promises protection, He also calls His people to actively refute false accusations, implying a partnership between divine protection and human responsibility.
4. Spiritual warfare: this verse acknowledges the reality of spiritual attacks but assures believers of ultimate victory in Christ.

When applying this verse to our lives, we should see it as an encouragement to trust in God's protection and to use our words to stand firm against lies and accusations, whether from external sources or our own negative self-talk.

Balancing faith declarations with inner healing

While faith declarations and positive confessions can be powerful tools in our spiritual journey, they must be balanced with the deep work of inner healing. Simply speaking positive words without addressing underlying wounds and beliefs can lead to superficial change at best or denial and suppression of real issues at worst.

Here are some principles for balancing faith declarations with inner healing:

1. Acknowledge the pain: before rushing to positive declarations, it's important to acknowledge and process our hurts and traumas. The Psalms provide a beautiful example of honest lament combined with declarations of trust in God.
2. Seek root causes: look beyond symptoms to understand the root causes of negative patterns in your life. This may

involve counseling, prayer ministry, or deep personal reflection.

3. Align declarations with truth: ensure that your faith declarations are grounded in biblical truth, not just wishful thinking. Meditate on Scripture to renew your mind (Romans 12:2).

4. Practice authenticity: be honest with God and yourself and trust others about your struggles. Authentic faith admits weaknesses while trusting in God's strength.

5. Embrace the process: healing and transformation are often gradual processes. Combine faith declarations with patient endurance and trust in God's timing.

6. Address false beliefs: identify and challenge false beliefs about yourself, others, and God that may be hindering your healing and growth.

7. Cultivate a lifestyle of praise: regular praise and thanksgiving can shift our focus from problems to God's faithfulness, creating fertile ground for positive change.

8. Community support: share your journey with a supportive community that can encourage you, pray for you, and hold you accountable.

9. Professional help: don't hesitate to seek professional counseling or therapy when needed, especially for deep-seated traumas or persistent mental health challenges.

10. Holistic approach: remember that healing involves the spirit, soul, and body. Care for your physical health, engage in spiritual disciplines, and nurture healthy relationships.

The power of words is a profound biblical truth that can play a significant role in our journey from victimhood to victory. Our speech has the potential to shape our reality, influence our mindset, and even impact our spiritual battles. However, we must approach this power with wisdom, understanding the balance between faith declarations and the necessary work of inner healing.

Let us hold fast to the truth of Ephesians 4:29: "Do not let any unwholesome talk come out of your mouths, but only what is helpful for building others up according to their needs, that it may benefit those who listen." May our words be a source of life, healing, and encouragement—both to ourselves and to those around us.

By embracing the power of words in a balanced, biblical way, we can partner with God in the transformative work he wants to do in our lives. As we speak truth over our circumstances, refute lies with God's Word, and engage in the deep work of inner healing, we position ourselves to experience the fullness of the wholeness and freedom that Christ offers.

Generational Curses and Ancestral Sins

Discussion on generational curses and ancestral sins has long been a topic of discussion and concern in many Christian circles. It touches on deep questions about the nature of sin, the justice of God, and the extent to which we are influenced by the actions of our forebears. As we proceed in our discussion on being whole, there is a need to understand the biblical foundations for generational curses, learn how to identify generational patterns, discuss ways to break free from ancestral sins, and understand the crucial role of forgiveness in breaking these cycles.

Biblical understanding of generational influences

The idea of generational influences is not new; it has roots in both the Old and New Testaments. To understand this concept biblically, we need to examine several key passages and principles.

1. (Exodus 20:5–6 and Deuteronomy 5:9–10) These passages, part of the Ten Commandments, state that God punishes the children for the sin of the parents to the third and fourth generation of those who hate him but shows love to a thousand generations of those who love Him and keep His commandments. This verse has often been cited as evidence for generational curses.
2. (Ezekiel 18:20) However, this verse seems to contradict the idea of generational punishment: "The one who sins is the one who will die. The child will not share the guilt of the

WILT THOU BE MADE WHOLE?

parent, nor will the parent share the guilt of the child." This passage emphasizes individual responsibility for sin.

3. (Jeremiah 31:29–30) Similarly, these verses state, "In those days people will no longer say, 'The parents have eaten sour grapes, and the children's teeth are set on edge.' Instead, everyone will die for their own sin; whoever eats sour grapes—their own teeth will be set on edge."

4. (Romans 5:12–21) This passage discusses how sin entered the world through one man (Adam) and affected all of humanity, but also how righteousness and life came through one man (Jesus Christ).

Reconciling these passages requires careful interpretation. While God doesn't punish children for their parents' sins in a direct, judicial sense, the consequences of sin often affect subsequent generations. This influence can be seen in various ways:

- Learned behaviors and attitudes
- Environmental factors
- Genetic predispositions
- Spiritual influences

It's important to note that while these influences can be strong, they do not determine an individual's destiny. Each person is ultimately responsible for their own choices and relationship with God.

Identifying generational patterns in your life

Recognizing generational patterns is a crucial step in addressing and breaking free from negative cycles. Here are some ways to identify these patterns:

1. *Family history analysis*: study your family tree and look for recurring issues such as addiction, abuse, divorce, or specific health problems. Pay attention to stories and anecdotes passed down through generations.

2. *Behavioral patterns*: observe repeated behaviors or reactions in yourself that mirror those of your parents or grandparents. Notice how you handle stress, conflict, or relationships compared to your family members.
3. *Belief systems*: examine your core beliefs about money, success, relationships, or self-worth. Consider how these beliefs align with or differ from those of your family.
4. *Emotional tendencies*: reflect on dominant emotions in your family (e.g., anger, fear, shame). Identify any emotional struggles you face that seem to echo through your family history.
5. *Spiritual Patterns*: Look at the spiritual or religious practices (or lack thereof) in your family lineage. Consider any repetitive spiritual struggles or areas of resistance.
6. *Health patterns*: Note any recurring health issues that seem to run in the family. Consider both physical and mental health patterns.
7. *Relationship dynamics*: observe how relationships (marital, parental, sibling) tend to function in your family. Look for patterns of communication, conflict resolution, or attachment styles.
8. *Career and financial patterns*: examine trends in career choices, work ethics, or financial management across generations.
9. *Addictive behaviors*: identify any recurring addictive tendencies in your family line (substances, behaviors, etc.).
10. *Trauma patterns*: look for repeated experiences of trauma or ways of coping with trauma across generations.

It's important to approach this analysis with compassion and objectivity. The goal is not to assign blame but to gain understanding and awareness as a first step toward positive change.

WILT THOU BE MADE WHOLE?

Breaking free from ancestral sins

Breaking free from ancestral sins involves a multifaceted approach that combines spiritual, psychological, and practical strategies. Here are some key steps:

1. Acknowledgment and repentance

    - Recognize the patterns and sins that have affected your family line.
    - Take personal responsibility for your own participation in these patterns.
    - Repent sincerely before God, asking for His forgiveness and cleansing.

2. Renunciation

    - Verbally renounce any involvement or agreement with ancestral sins.
    - Declare your intention to break free from these patterns in Jesus's name.

3. Claim your new identity in Christ

    - Affirm your position as a new creation in Christ (2 Corinthians 5:17).
    - Meditate on scriptures that speak of your identity as a child of God.

4. Break ungodly soul ties

    - Pray to sever any unhealthy spiritual connections to ancestors or family members.
    - Ask God to heal any areas where these connections have influenced you negatively.

5. Deliverance prayer

   - Seek prayer support from mature believers.
   - Pray for deliverance from any demonic influences associated with ancestral sins.

6. Renew your mind

   - Actively replace negative thought patterns with biblical truths.
   - Engage in regular Bible study and meditation on God's Word.

7. Seek healing for emotional wounds

   - Pursue inner healing prayer or Christian counseling to address deep-seated issues.
   - Allow God to heal areas of hurt, rejection, or trauma.

8. Establish new patterns

   - Consciously make choices that align with God's Word and break old cycles.
   - Develop new habits and behaviors that reflect your freedom in Christ.

9. Join a supportive community

   - Surround yourself with believers who can encourage and support your journey.
   - Be accountable to trusted individuals who can help you maintain your freedom.

WILT THOU BE MADE WHOLE?

10. Walk in vigilance

   - Stay alert to any attempts of the enemy to draw you back into old patterns.
   - Maintain a consistent prayer life and spiritual discipline.

11. Extend grace to your family

   - While setting healthy boundaries, extend grace and forgiveness to family members still struggling with these issues.
   - Be a positive influence without taking responsibility for others' choices.

12. Seek professional help when needed

   - Don't hesitate to seek professional Christian counseling or therapy for deep-seated issues.
   - Recognize that breaking generational patterns often requires both spiritual and psychological work.

The Journey to Wholeness

In our walk with Christ, we often hear about the promise of abundant life (John 10:10) and the transformative power of faith (2 Corinthians 5:17). Yet for many believers, the reality of daily life can feel far from these lofty ideals. Past traumas, self-doubt, and a distorted self-image can create barriers that seem insurmountable. However, the journey to wholeness is not only possible but essential for living out the fullness of God's plan for our lives.

The path to wholeness is a deeply personal and often challenging journey. It requires us to confront the wounds of our past, challenge the negative beliefs we've internalized, and courageously step into a new identity rooted in Christ. This process isn't about achieving perfection or eliminating all struggles; rather, it's about embracing our full humanity while allowing God's healing power to work in every aspect of our being.

We must recognize that wholeness is not a destination but a continual process of growth and transformation. It involves learning to see ourselves through God's eyes, understanding our inherent worth as His beloved children, and living from a place of authenticity and vulnerability. This journey may bring us face to face with the pain we've long buried, but it also opens the door to profound healing and freedom.

Ultimately, the pursuit of wholeness is an act of faith and obedience. It's a declaration that we believe in God's promises of restoration and renewal, even when our circumstances or feelings suggest otherwise.

WILT THOU BE MADE WHOLE?

Acknowledging past traumas

The journey to wholeness begins with a crucial, often challenging step: acknowledging the wounds we carry. In our fast-paced, success-driven society, we've become masters at suppressing pain, putting on brave faces, and convincing ourselves that our past hurts weren't significant or that we should simply "move on." However, true healing can only commence when we courageously face our pain with honesty—both in our relationship with ourselves and with God.

The cost of denial

Denying or minimizing our past traumas can have severe consequences. When we bury our pain, it doesn't disappear; instead, it often manifests in unhealthy ways:

1. Emotional numbness: we may find ourselves unable to experience joy or connect deeply with others fully.
2. Unexplained anxiety or depression: unresolved trauma can lead to persistent mental health challenges.
3. Physical symptoms: our bodies often carry the burden of unacknowledged pain, resulting in various physical ailments.
4. Relationship difficulties: unhealed wounds can affect our ability to trust and form healthy connections.
5. Spiritual stagnation: unaddressed pain can create barriers in our relationship with God.

Biblical examples of honesty in pain

Scripture provides us with numerous examples of individuals who didn't shy away from expressing their pain to God. Their raw honesty serves as a model for us:

1. David: As mentioned, David's psalms are filled with honest expressions of anguish, fear, and even anger. In Psalms

13:1–2, he cries out, "How long, O Lord? Will you forget me forever? How long will you hide your face from me? How long must I wrestle with my thoughts and day after day have sorrow in my heart?"

2. Job: In the midst of immense suffering, Job didn't hesitate to voice his pain and confusion to God. In Job 3:11, he laments, "Why did I not perish at birth, and die as I came from the womb?"

3. Jeremiah: Known as the "weeping prophet," Jeremiah openly expressed his sorrow over the state of his people. In Jeremiah 20:18, he questions, "Why did I ever come out of the womb to see trouble and sorrow and to end my days in shame?"

4. Jesus: Even Jesus, in his humanity, expressed his anguish openly. In the Garden of Gethsemane, he told his disciples, "My soul is overwhelmed with sorrow to the point of death" (Matthew 26:38).

These biblical figures demonstrate that expressing our pain to God is not only acceptable but can be a profound act of faith and trust.

Practical steps for acknowledging past traumas

1. Journaling

   o Set aside dedicated time for reflection and writing.
   o Start with recent experiences and gradually work backward.
   o Be specific about events, your feelings, and physical sensations you experienced.
   o Don't censor yourself; allow all thoughts and emotions to flow freely onto the page.
   o Consider using prompts like "The hardest part about that experience was…" or "If I could speak to my younger self in that moment, I would say…"

2. Seeking counsel

- o Seek Christian counselors or therapists in your area who specialize in trauma.
- o Prepare for your first session by writing down key experiences or issues you want to address.
- o Be patient with the process; healing often takes time and may involve revisiting painful memories.
- o Remember that seeking help is a sign of strength, not weakness.

3. Prayer

- o Start by asking the Holy Spirit to guide and comfort you as you face your pain.
- o Use the Psalms as a model for expressing your emotions honestly to God.
- o Try prayer journaling, writing letters to God, and expressing your hurt, anger, or confusion.
- o Practice listening to prayer, allowing space for God to speak to your heart.

4. Support groups

- o Research Christian support groups in your area or online communities focused on healing from trauma.
- o Start by listening to others' stories before sharing your own.
- o Remember that vulnerability often encourages vulnerability in others.
- o Respect the confidentiality of the group to create a safe space for all members.

The purpose of acknowledgment

It's crucial to understand that acknowledging past traumas isn't about dwelling in pain or victimhood. Rather, it's about bringing hidden things into the light where God's healing power can work. As 1 John 1:7 reminds us, "But if we walk in the light, as he is in the light, we have fellowship with one another, and the blood of Jesus, his Son, purifies us from all sin."

Acknowledging our wounds allows us to do the following:

1. Identify patterns of behavior or thinking that stem from past hurt.
2. Release the energy we've been using to suppress painful memories.
3. Open ourselves to God's comfort and healing presence.
4. Develop empathy for others who are hurting.
5. Break generational cycles of trauma and dysfunction.

Confronting self-doubt and low self-esteem

The journey from acknowledging past traumas to healing is often paved with self-doubt and low self-esteem. These negative beliefs about ourselves can feel like an immovable part of our identity, deeply rooted in our psyche. They whisper lies that contradict the truth of who God says we are.

Scripture paints a beautiful picture of our worth in God's eyes. Psalm 139:14 tells us we are "fearfully and wonderfully made," a testament to God's intentional and masterful creation of each individual. Ephesians 2:10 goes further, declaring us God's "masterpiece," or "poiema" in Greek—his work of art. Jeremiah 31:3 assures us of God's "everlasting love," a love that transcends time and circumstance.

Yet internalizing these truths can be a daily struggle. Our experiences, the words of others, and the enemy's lies can create a chasm between God's view of us and our view of ourselves. Bridging this gap requires intentional effort and a willingness to challenge long-held beliefs.

WILT THOU BE MADE WHOLE?

Strategies for confronting self-doubt and building healthy self-esteem:

1.   Identify negative self-talk:

Our internal dialogue shapes our reality more than we often realize. The first step in combating negative self-talk is becoming aware of it. Start by paying close attention to your thoughts throughout the day. You might be surprised at how often you criticize yourself.

Exercise: For one week, keep a "thought journal." Jot down negative thoughts as they occur. At the end of the week, review your entries. Look for patterns. Are there specific triggers? Times of day when negative thoughts are more prevalent?

Ask yourself: Would I speak to a friend this way? Often, we're much harsher with ourselves than we would ever be with others. Recognizing this discrepancy can be eye-opening.

2.   Challenge distorted thinking:

Once you've identified negative self-talk, it's time to challenge it. This process, often used in cognitive-behavioral therapy, involves examining your thoughts critically.

When you catch yourself in negative self-talk, pause and ask three important questions:

- Is this thought true? Often, our negative self-talk is based on assumptions or distortions, not facts.
- Is this thought helpful? Even if there's a grain of truth, dwelling on it may not be constructive.
- Is this thought aligned with what God says about me? This is crucial. Our thoughts should be held up against the standard of God's Word.

Exercise: Create a "thought challenge" worksheet. Write down a negative thought, then answer each of the three questions. Finally, reframe the thought in a more balanced, God-centered way.

3. Meditate on scripture:

Surrounding yourself with God's truth is a powerful antidote to negative self-talk. Choose verses that specifically address your struggles with self-worth.

Some powerful verses to consider:

- First Peter 2:9 says, "But you are a chosen people, a royal priesthood, a holy nation, God's special possession."
- Romans 8:1 says, "There is now no condemnation for those who are in Christ Jesus."
- Zephaniah 3:17 says, "The Lord your God is with you, the Mighty Warrior who saves. He will take great delight in you; in his love, he will no longer rebuke you, but will rejoice over you with singing."

Exercise: Create a "truth arsenal." Write these verses on index cards. Place them where you'll see them often—on your mirror, in your car, as bookmarks. Set reminders on your phone to read them throughout the day.

4. Practice self-compassion:

Self-compassion involves treating ourselves with the same kindness and understanding we'd offer a close friend. It's not about excusing mistakes but about responding to our failures and struggles with grace rather than harsh criticism.

Exercise: When you're facing a difficulty or have made a mistake, pause and ask, "How would I comfort a friend in this situation?" Then offer those same words of comfort to yourself.

Remember, God's love for us is not dependent on our performance. Romans 5:8 reminds us that Christ died for us "While we were still sinners."

WILT THOU BE MADE WHOLE?

5. Set realistic goals:

Setting and achieving goals, no matter how small, can significantly boost our self-esteem. The key is to make these goals realistic and achievable.

Exercise: Use the SMART goal framework (Specific, Measurable, Achievable, Relevant, Time-bound) to set daily or weekly goals. Start small. Accomplishing a series of small goals builds momentum and confidence.

Celebrate your successes, no matter how minor they might seem. Each achievement is a step toward a healthier self-image.

6. Serve others:

Serving others can profoundly impact our self-esteem. It shifts our focus outward, allowing us to see the positive impact we can have on the world around us.

Exercise: Look for opportunities to serve in your church or community. It could be as simple as offering to pray for a friend or helping a neighbor with a task. Pay attention to how serving others makes you feel about yourself.

Remember Galatians 6:9–10: "Let us not become weary in doing good, for at the proper time we will reap a harvest if we do not give up. Therefore, as we have opportunity, let us do good to all people, especially to those who belong to the family of believers."

Building healthy self-esteem is a journey, not a destination. It's about gradually aligning our self-perception with God's view of us. This doesn't mean we'll never struggle or make mistakes. Rather, it means we learn to see ourselves as God sees us—beloved children work in progress, valued not for our performance but for our inherent worth as His creation.

As you work on building your self-esteem, remember that this process is part of your spiritual growth. It's about learning to see yourself through God's eyes, embracing both His love for you and His desire for you to grow and mature in Christ. Your worth is not determined by your accomplishments or failures but by the immeasurable price God paid for you through His Son, Jesus Christ.

Embracing vulnerability and authenticity

In a world that often values strength and self-sufficiency, embracing vulnerability can feel counterintuitive. Yet, it's in our weakness that God's strength is perfected (2 Corinthians 12:9). True authenticity—being real about our struggles, doubts, and failures—creates space for genuine connection and growth.

Jesus himself modeled vulnerability. In the Garden of Gethsemane, he shared his anguish with his disciples, saying, "My soul is overwhelmed with sorrow to the point of death" (Matthew 26:38). If the Son of God could be honest about his struggles, how much more should we?

Here are some ways to cultivate vulnerability and authenticity:

1. Start small: Begin by sharing something mildly uncomfortable with a trusted friend. As you build trust and confidence, you can gradually open up about deeper issues.
2. Be honest in prayer: God already knows everything about us, so there's no need to pretend. Pour out your heart to Him, just as the Psalmists did.
3. Join a small group: Find a group of believers where you can share openly and support one another.
4. Practice active listening: When others are vulnerable with you, listen without judgment. This creates a safe space for authenticity to flourish.
5. Embrace imperfection: Remember that authenticity isn't about having it all together. It's about being real about your journey, including the stumbles and falls.
6. Share your testimony: Your story of God's work in your life, including the messy parts, can be a powerful encouragement to others.

WILT THOU BE MADE WHOLE?

Brené Brown, a researcher on vulnerability, says, "Vulnerability is the birthplace of innovation, creativity, and change." As we learn to be vulnerable and authentic, we open ourselves up to deeper relationships, personal growth, and a more intimate walk with God.

Developing a healthy self-image rooted in Christ

The culmination of our journey to wholeness is developing a healthy self-image that is firmly rooted in Christ. This doesn't mean we'll never struggle with doubts or insecurities, but it does mean that our fundamental understanding of who we are is based on God's truth rather than the world's lies or our past experiences.

Paul writes in Galatians 2:20, "I have been crucified with Christ and I no longer live, but Christ lives in me. The life I now live in the body, I live by faith in the Son of God, who loved me and gave himself for me." This verse encapsulates the essence of a Christ-centered self-image.

Here are some key aspects of developing a healthy, Christ-rooted self-image:

1. Understanding our new identity: In Christ, we are new creations (2 Corinthians 5:17). We are no longer defined by our past sins, failures, or the labels others have placed on us.
2. Embracing God's love: Our worth is not based on our performance or others' opinions but on the unchanging love of God. Romans 8:38–39 assures us that nothing can separate us from this love.
3. Recognizing our purpose: We are created for good works (Ephesians 2:10). Understanding that we have a unique role in God's plan gives us a sense of value and direction.
4. Balancing humility and confidence: A healthy self-image involves both humility (recognizing our dependence on God) and confidence (trusting in the abilities God has given us).

5. Seeing ourselves as part of the body of Christ: We are not isolated individuals but part of a larger community. Our self-image should include our role in the church and how we contribute to the body of believers.
6. Embracing growth: A healthy self-image doesn't mean thinking we're perfect. It means being secure enough to acknowledge our areas of weakness and actively work on them.
7. Practicing gratitude: Regularly thanking God for who He is and what He's done in our lives helps shift our focus from our shortcomings to His goodness.

Practical steps for developing this Christ-centered self-image might include:

- Daily affirmations based on Scripture: Start each day by declaring God's truths over your life.
- Serving in areas of giftedness: Use your God-given talents to serve others, reinforcing your sense of purpose.
- Regular self-reflection: Take time to examine your thoughts and actions in light of God's Word.
- Accountability partnerships: Find a mature believer who can help you see yourself accurately and encourage your growth.
- Celebrating progress: Acknowledge the ways God is working in your life, no matter how small they might seem.

Remember, developing a healthy self-image is a lifelong process. There will be setbacks and struggles along the way. The key is to keep returning to the truth of who God says you are.

The journey to wholeness is not a straight path. It involves acknowledging past traumas, confronting self-doubt, embracing vulnerability, and developing a healthy self-image rooted in Christ. This journey requires courage, perseverance, and, most importantly, a willingness to let God work in the deepest parts of our hearts.

WILT THOU BE MADE WHOLE?

As you walk this path, remember the words of Philippians 1:6: "Being confident of this, that he who began a good work in you will carry it on to completion until the day of Christ Jesus." God is not finished with you yet. He is faithfully working to restore, heal, and transform you into the whole, vibrant person He created you to be.

Your journey to wholeness is not just for your own benefit. As you experience healing and transformation, you become better equipped to minister to others, to share your story, and to reflect God's love to a broken world. Your wholeness becomes a testament to God's redeeming power and a beacon of hope for those still struggling.

So take heart, beloved child of God. The journey may be challenging, but it is worth it. With each step towards wholeness, you are becoming more fully the person God designed you to be—fully loved, fully accepted, and fully alive in Christ.

Practical Steps for Healing

The journey of healing from trauma and overcoming challenges is both deeply personal and profoundly transformative. While the path to wholeness may seem daunting, there are practical steps you can take to facilitate your healing process, and the first of them is seeking help through counseling.

Seeking professional help is a crucial step in the healing process. Many people hesitate to reach out, fearing stigma or believing they should be able to overcome their struggles alone. However, professional counseling can provide invaluable support and guidance.

Trained therapists and counselors possess the skills and knowledge to help you navigate the complex emotions and thought patterns that often accompany trauma. They can offer evidence-based techniques and strategies tailored to your specific needs, helping you process your experiences in a safe and supportive environment.

Professional help is particularly important when dealing with trauma, as it can manifest in various ways, including post-traumatic stress disorder (PTSD), anxiety, depression, or other mental health challenges. A qualified professional can accurately diagnose these conditions and provide appropriate treatment.

Moreover, counseling can help you develop coping mechanisms, improve your self-awareness, and learn how to reframe negative thought patterns. These skills are essential in breaking free from the victim mentality and moving towards a more empowered perspective.

Seeking help is not a sign of weakness but a courageous step towards healing and growth. It demonstrates your commitment to your well-being and your determination to overcome the challenges you face.

WILT THOU BE MADE WHOLE?

Developing a strong support system

While professional help is crucial, the importance of a strong support system cannot be overstated. Surrounding yourself with understanding, compassionate individuals can provide emotional sustenance and practical assistance throughout your healing journey.

A robust support system may include the following:

1. Family members: Those who offer unconditional love and support can be a cornerstone of your healing process. However, it's important to recognize that not all family relationships are healthy. Choose to lean on those who uplift and encourage you.
2. Friends: Trusted friends can offer a listening ear, share burdens, and provide moments of joy and laughter—all vital components of healing.
3. Support groups: Connecting with others who have similar experiences can be incredibly validating and educational. These groups offer a sense of community and the opportunity to both give and receive support.
4. Church community: For many, their faith community provides a sense of belonging and spiritual support. Fellow believers can offer prayer, encouragement, and practical assistance.
5. Mentors: Having someone who has walked a similar path and emerged stronger can provide hope and guidance. A mentor can share wisdom from their own experiences and offer a perspective that comes from having navigated similar challenges.

Building and maintaining a support system requires effort and vulnerability. It involves being open about your struggles, asking for help when needed, and being willing to receive support. This process can be challenging, especially if past experiences have led to trust issues. However, the benefits of a strong support network are immeasurable in your journey towards wholeness.

Spiritual disciplines for inner healing

For many, faith plays a central role in the healing process. Engaging in spiritual disciplines can provide comfort, strength, and a sense of purpose. These practices can help reframe your experiences within a larger context of faith and hope. Let's explore some key spiritual disciplines that can contribute to inner healing:

1. Prayer and meditation

Prayer is a powerful tool for healing. It provides a direct line of communication with God, allowing you to express your deepest fears, pains, and hopes. Through prayer, you can:

- Pour out your heart to God, knowing He hears and understands.
- Find peace in God's presence, even amidst turmoil.
- Seek wisdom and guidance for your healing journey.
- Experience God's love and acceptance, countering feelings of shame or unworthiness.

Meditation, particularly on Scripture or godly principles, can help calm your mind and refocus your thoughts. It can involve the following:

- Quietly reflecting on a Bible verse or passage.
- Practicing mindfulness, being present in the moment, and being aware of God's presence.
- Visualizing healing and wholeness, anchored in God's promises.

Regular prayer and meditation can help reshape your thought patterns, reduce anxiety, and foster a deeper sense of peace and trust in God's plan for your life.

WILT THOU BE MADE WHOLE?

2. Scripture study and memorization

The Bible offers comfort, wisdom, and guidance for every aspect of life, including healing from trauma. Engaging deeply with Scripture can be as follows:

- Provide truth to counter lies you may have believed about yourself or your situation.
- Offer examples of others who have overcome adversity through faith.
- Reveal God's character and His promises for your life.
- Equip you with wisdom for navigating challenges.

Scripture memorization is particularly powerful. By internalizing God's Word, you have a ready resource to draw upon in moments of distress or doubt. Some verses that many find comforting in times of healing include:

- "The Lord is close to the brokenhearted and saves those who are crushed in spirit" (Psalm 34:18).
- "He heals the brokenhearted and binds up their wounds" (Psalm 147:3).
- "For I know the plans I have for you," declares the Lord, "plans to prosper you and not to harm you, plans to give you hope and a future" (Jeremiah 29:11).

Consider starting a habit of daily Bible reading, perhaps following a devotional guide or a Bible-in-a-year plan. As you read, reflect on how the passages apply to your life and your healing journey.

3. Worship and praise

Worship and praise shift our focus from our circumstances to God's greatness, power, and love. This shift in perspective can be tremendously healing. Through worship, we:

- Acknowledge God's sovereignty over our lives, including our pain and struggles.
- Express gratitude, which can help counter negative emotions.
- Experience joy and peace in God's presence.
- Connect with God on an emotional level, allowing for deep inner healing.

Worship can take many forms:

- Singing or listening to worship music.
- Creating art as an act of worship.
- Spending time in nature, marveling at God's creation.
- Serving others as an expression of love for God.

Make worship a regular part of your life, not just a Sunday morning activity. Let it permeate your daily routines, becoming a lifestyle that continually draws you closer to God and further along your path of healing.

Setting healthy boundaries

An essential aspect of healing and maintaining emotional health is setting and enforcing healthy boundaries. Boundaries are the limits we set with others to protect our physical and emotional well-being. For those healing from trauma, establishing boundaries is crucial for several reasons:

1. Self-protection: boundaries help protect you from further harm or re-traumatization.

WILT THOU BE MADE WHOLE?

2. Emotional regulation: they allow you to manage your emotional energy and avoid becoming overwhelmed.
3. Self-respect: setting boundaries demonstrates that you value yourself and your well-being.
4. Healthy relationships: clear boundaries foster more honest, respectful relationships.

Here are some steps to help you set healthy boundaries:

1. Self-awareness: recognize your limits—physical, emotional, and spiritual. What situations or behaviors make you uncomfortable or stressed?
2. Clear communication: express your boundaries clearly and calmly. Use "I" statements to convey your needs without blaming others.
3. Consistency: enforce your boundaries consistently. People will learn to respect your limits when you uphold them consistently.
4. Start small: if setting boundaries is new to you, start with smaller, less emotionally charged issues before tackling more significant ones.
5. Expect resistance: some people may push back against your new boundaries. Stay firm, and remember that you have the right to protect your well-being.
6. Self-care: prioritize self-care as you navigate this process. Setting boundaries can be challenging and may bring up difficult emotions.
7. Forgiveness: remember that setting boundaries is not about punishing others but about taking care of yourself. Practice forgiveness, both for others and for yourself.

Examples of healthy boundaries might include the following:

- Limiting contact with individuals who are harmful to your emotional health

- Saying no to additional commitments when you're feeling overwhelmed
- Expressing your needs and feelings honestly in relationships
- Taking time for yourself to recharge, even if others demand your attention

Remember, setting boundaries is a skill that improves with practice. Be patient with yourself as you learn and grow in this area.

The journey of healing from trauma and breaking free from a victim mentality is multifaceted, requiring attention to various aspects of your life—emotional, relational, and spiritual. By seeking professional help, developing a strong support system, engaging in spiritual disciplines, and setting healthy boundaries, you are taking significant steps toward wholeness.

Remember that healing is a process, not a destination. There may be setbacks along the way, but each step forward is a victory. Be patient and compassionate with yourself as you navigate this journey. Trust in God's love and guidance, and hold onto hope for the future He has planned for you.

As you implement these practical steps, you'll likely find that they reinforce each other. Professional counseling can help you develop better boundaries. A strong support system can encourage you in your spiritual disciplines. Worship and praise can deepen your relationships within your support network.

Embrace this holistic approach to healing, and trust that with time, effort, and faith, you can break free from the victim spirit and step into the wholeness and purpose God has for you.

Overcoming Obstacles in the Healing Process

The journey of healing from trauma and breaking free from a victim mentality is seldom a straight path. As we progress, we often encounter obstacles that can challenge our resolve and test our faith. However, these hurdles are not insurmountable, and with God's grace and guidance, we can overcome them.

There may be days when old wounds feel fresh or past behaviors resurface, leaving us feeling discouraged and doubtful of our progress. It's crucial to remember that healing is not linear, and temporary setbacks do not negate the growth we've achieved.

1. Recognizing setbacks as opportunities for growth

The apostle Paul reminds us in Romans 5:3–4, "Not only so, but we also glory in our sufferings, because we know that suffering produces perseverance; perseverance, character; and character, hope." When we encounter setbacks, we can choose to view them as opportunities to deepen our faith and strengthen our resilience.

Practical steps:

- Journal about your setbacks, identifying triggers and patterns.
- Reflect on lessons learned from each challenge.
- Share your struggles with a trusted friend or counselor.

2. Combating discouragement with truth

Discouragement often stems from believing lies about ourselves or our situation. Counteract these negative thoughts with the truth of God's Word. Philippians 4:8 instructs us, "Finally, brothers and sisters, whatever is true, whatever is noble, whatever is right, whatever is pure, whatever is lovely, whatever is admirable—if anything is excellent or praiseworthy—think about such things."

Practical steps:

- Memorize and meditate on encouraging Scripture verses.
- Create a "truth journal" to combat negative self-talk
- Surround yourself with positive, faith-filled individuals.

3. Embracing God's grace in weakness

Remember that our strength comes not from ourselves but from God. As Paul writes in 2 Corinthians 12:9, "But he said to me, 'My grace is sufficient for you, for my power is made perfect in weakness.' Therefore I will boast all the more gladly about my weaknesses, so that Christ's power may rest on me."

Practical steps:

- Practice daily surrender to God, acknowledging your need for his strength.
- Celebrate small victories and progress, no matter how minor they may seem.
- Seek support from your church community or a Christian support group.

Addressing ongoing negative relationships

Healing becomes particularly challenging when we remain in contact with individuals who have hurt us or continue to reinforce negative patterns in our lives. While forgiveness is a crucial aspect of

Christian faith, it doesn't always mean maintaining close relationships with those who have caused harm.

1. Setting healthy boundaries

Boundaries are essential for protecting our emotional and spiritual well-being. Jesus himself set boundaries, as we see in Luke 4:28–30 when He walked away from an angry crowd. Establishing and maintaining healthy boundaries is an act of stewardship over the life God has given us.

Practical steps:

- Identify relationships that hinder your healing process.
- Communicate your boundaries clearly and firmly.
- Be prepared to enforce consequences if boundaries are crossed.

2. Practicing forgiveness without compromising safety

Forgiveness is a cornerstone of the Christian faith, but it doesn't require us to place ourselves in harmful situations. Matthew 10:16 advises, "I am sending you out like sheep among wolves. Therefore be as shrewd as snakes and as innocent as doves."

Practical steps:

- Pray for those who have hurt you, releasing them to God's justice.
- Seek counsel from a pastor or Christian therapist about complex relational issues.
- Consider limiting or ending contact with consistently toxic individuals.

3. Surrounding yourself with positive influences

Proverbs 13:20 tells us, "Walk with the wise and become wise, for a companion of fools suffers harm." As you heal, it's crucial to cultivate relationships that support your growth and encourage your faith.

Practical steps:

- Join a Bible study or support group focused on healing.
- Seek mentorship from mature Christians who have overcome similar challenges.
- Volunteer or engage in community service to build new, positive relationships.

Navigating triggers and painful memories

Triggers and painful memories can often feel like roadblocks in our healing journey. They may arise unexpectedly, causing us to relive traumatic experiences or fall back into negative thought patterns. However, with God's help and intentional strategies, we can learn to manage these challenges effectively.

1. Identifying and understanding your triggers

Self-awareness is key to managing triggers. By recognizing what situations, words, or environments tend to provoke negative reactions, we can better prepare ourselves and develop coping strategies.

Practical steps:

- Keep a trigger journal to track patterns and common themes.
- Work with a Christian counselor to unpack the root causes of your triggers.
- Practice mindfulness to become more aware of your emotional responses.

2. Developing healthy coping mechanisms

When triggers arise, having a toolkit of healthy coping strategies can help us navigate the emotional storm. Isaiah 26:3 reminds

WILT THOU BE MADE WHOLE?

us, "You will keep in perfect peace those whose minds are steadfast, because they trust in you."

Practical steps:

- Create a "grounding kit" with sensory items that help you stay present.
- Develop a list of Scripture verses or prayers to recite when triggered.
- Learn and practice relaxation techniques like deep breathing or progressive muscle relaxation.

3. Reframing painful memories through God's perspective

While we cannot change the past, we can change how we view it. Romans 8:28 assures us, "And we know that in all things God works for the good of those who love him, who have been called according to his purpose."

Practical steps:

- Practice gratitude, focusing on how God has brought you through difficult times.
- Engage in trauma-informed therapies like Eye Movement Desensitization and Reprocessing (EMDR) or cognitive processing therapy with a Christian counselor.
- Write a letter to your past self, offering comfort and wisdom from your current perspective.

4. Embracing the healing power of lament

The Bible is full of examples of lament, where God's people cry out to Him in their pain. Lament allows us to honestly express our hurt while still turning towards God in faith. Psalm 62:8 encourages us, "*Trust in him at all times, you people; pour out your hearts to him, for God is our refuge.*"

Practical steps:

- Study and pray through Psalms of lament.
- Write your own laments, expressing your pain to God.
- Share your laments with trusted friends or in a support group setting.

The role of perseverance and patience

Healing is often a long process that requires sustained effort and unwavering faith. The virtues of perseverance and patience are crucial as we navigate the ups and downs of recovery.

1. Understanding the nature of long-term healing

Instant transformation is rare; most often, healing occurs gradually over time. Galatians 6:9 encourages us, "Let us not become weary in doing good, for at the proper time we will reap a harvest if we do not give up."

2. Cultivating perseverance through spiritual disciplines

Spiritual disciplines like prayer, Bible study, and fasting can strengthen our resolve and deepen our connection with God. James 1:2–4 tells us, "Consider it pure joy, my brothers and sisters, whenever you face trials of many kinds, because you know that the testing of your faith produces perseverance. Let perseverance finish its work so that you may be mature and complete, not lacking anything."

3. Embracing God's timing and sovereignty

While we may desire immediate healing, it's important to trust in God's perfect timing. Ecclesiastes 3:11 reminds us, "He has made everything beautiful in its time. He has also set eternity in the human heart; yet no one can fathom what God has done from beginning to end."

WILT THOU BE MADE WHOLE?

4. Building a support system for the long haul

Healing is not meant to be a solitary journey. Ecclesiastes 4:9–10 tells us, "Two are better than one, because they have a good return for their labor: If either of them falls down, one can help the other up. But pity anyone who falls and has no one to help them up."

Overcoming obstacles in the healing process is an integral part of breaking free from the victim spirit and embracing the wholeness God intends for us. By addressing setbacks and discouragement, navigating difficult relationships, managing triggers and painful memories, and cultivating perseverance and patience, we position ourselves to receive the healing and restoration God offers.

Remember, you are not alone in this journey. *The God who began a good work in you will carry it on to completion* (Philippians 1:6). As you face obstacles, lean into His strength, trust His process, and remain open to the transformative work of the Holy Spirit in your life. Your story of healing and restoration will not only bring glory to God but will also serve as a beacon of hope for others on similar journeys.

Living in Victory

Embracing your identity in Christ is one of the crucial steps in the journey of breaking free from the victim spirit and living spirit. As believers, we are called to see ourselves not through the lens of our past experiences or current circumstances but through the truth of who God says we are.

Scripture tells us that in Christ, we are new creations (2 Corinthians 5:17). This means that our old identity, shaped by trauma and victimhood, no longer defines us. Instead, we have been given a new identity, one rooted in the love and acceptance of our Heavenly Father.

To fully embrace this identity, we must first understand what it means. In Christ, we are the following:

1. Chosen and beloved (Ephesians 1:4–5)
2. Forgiven and redeemed (Colossians 1:13–14)
3. Righteous and holy (2 Corinthians 5:21)
4. More than conquerors (Romans 8:37)
5. Children of God (John 1:12)

These truths are not mere platitudes but powerful declarations of who we are in God's eyes. When we begin to internalize these truths, they become a foundation for healing and transformation.

Practically speaking, embracing our identity in Christ involves:

1. Regular meditation on scripture: Spend time daily reading and reflecting on verses that speak to your identity in Christ.

WILT THOU BE MADE WHOLE?

2. Replacing negative self-talk with God's truth: When thoughts of unworthiness or victimhood arise, consciously replace them with what God says about you.
3. Surround yourself with believers who affirm your identity: Seek out a community that will remind you of who you are in Christ, especially during challenging times.
4. Acting in accordance with your new identity: Make decisions and behave in ways that align with who God says you are, even when you don't feel like it.
5. Praising God for your new identity: Regularly thank God for the new life and identity He has given you in Christ.

Remember, embracing your identity in Christ is not a one-time event but a continuous process. It requires persistence and patience. As you consistently align your thoughts and actions with the truth of who you are in Christ, you'll find that your perception of yourself and your circumstances will begin to shift. This new perspective becomes the foundation for moving from victim to victor.

From victim to victor: changing your narrative

The transition from victim to victor is a powerful journey of transformation that begins in the mind. It involves consciously changing the narrative of your life story from one of helplessness and defeat to one of strength and triumph.

As victims, we often define ourselves by what has happened to us. Our traumatic experiences become the central plot of our life story, coloring how we see ourselves and the world around us. However, as we embrace our identity in Christ, we gain the power to rewrite this narrative.

The first step in changing your narrative is recognizing that you have the authority to do so. Your past experiences are real, and their impact on your life is significant. However, they do not have the final say in defining who you are or what your future holds. As a child of God, you have been given the power to choose how you interpret and respond to your experiences.

59

Here are some practical steps to change your narrative:

1. Identify the current narrative: Take time to reflect on how you've been viewing your life story. What role have you assigned yourself? How have you interpreted the events of your life?

2. Challenge negative interpretations: Look at your experiences through the lens of God's love and sovereignty. How might God be using these experiences for your growth and His glory?

3. Reframe your experiences: Instead of seeing yourself as a passive victim of circumstances, view yourself as an overcomer who has survived and grown through challenges.

4. Focus on growth and lessons learned: Rather than dwelling on the pain of your experiences, concentrate on how they've made you stronger, wiser, or more compassionate.

5. Envision a new future: Based on your identity in Christ, create a vision for your life that's not limited by your past experiences.

6. Use empowering language: Pay attention to how you speak about yourself and your experiences. Replace victim language ("This always happens to me") with victor language ("I've overcome challenges before, and I can do it again").

7. Celebrate small victories: Acknowledge and celebrate the steps you're taking toward healing and growth, no matter how small they may seem.

Remember, changing your narrative doesn't mean denying or minimizing your past experiences. Instead, it means choosing to view them through the lens of God's redemptive power. It means recognizing that while you may have been a victim of circumstances, in Christ, you are ultimately a victor.

This shift in perspective is beautifully illustrated in the life of Joseph in the Old Testament. Despite being sold into slavery by his brothers and unjustly imprisoned, Joseph was able to see God's hand at work in his life. His powerful declaration to his brothers,

WILT THOU BE MADE WHOLE?

"You intended to harm me, but God intended it for good" (Genesis 50:20), is a perfect example of the victor's narrative.

As you continue to embrace your identity in Christ and change your narrative, you'll find yourself moving from a place of helplessness to one of empowerment. This new perspective will not only impact how you view yourself but also how you interact with the world around you.

Using your testimony to help others

As you progress on your journey from victim to victor, you'll discover that your experiences and growth can become a powerful tool to help others. Your testimony—the story of God's redemptive work in your life—has the potential to bring hope, healing, and transformation to those who are still struggling.

The Bible tells us in Revelation 12:11 that we are overcome by the blood of the Lamb and the word of our testimony. Your story of overcoming trauma and embracing your identity in Christ can be a beacon of light for others still trapped in darkness.

Here are some ways to effectively use your testimony to help others:

1. Share authentically: Be honest about your struggles and the reality of your journey. People are often more encouraged by real stories of gradual growth than by seemingly instantaneous transformations.
2. Focus on God's work: While it's important to acknowledge the challenges you've faced, the emphasis of your testimony should be on God's faithfulness, love, and power to heal and transform.
3. Offer hope: Highlight the positive changes in your life as a result of your healing journey. This can inspire hope in others that change is possible for them too.
4. Be sensitive: Recognize that everyone's journey is unique. While your experiences may resonate with others, avoid presenting your path as the only way to healing.

5. Use appropriate platforms: Look for opportunities to share your story in your church, support groups, or even through writing or speaking engagements.
6. Be prepared: Craft your testimony in a clear, concise manner that you can share in various time frames—from a few minutes to a longer presentation.
7. Pray for those who hear your story: Ask God to use your words to bring healing and hope to those who need it.

Remember, using your testimony to help others is not about having a perfect story or being fully "healed." It's about being willing to be vulnerable and to point others towards the God who brings beauty from ashes.

As you share your story, you may find that it not only helps others but also continues to strengthen your own faith and healing. There's something powerful about declaring God's faithfulness that reinforces our own belief in it.

Moreover, helping others can be a significant part of your own continued growth and healing. It allows you to see how far you've come and gives deeper meaning to your experiences. As you witness others finding hope through your story, it can further solidify your identity as a victor rather than a victim.

Forgiveness: The key to long-lasting freedom

Forgiveness is a crucial tool for achieving freedom. It allows the person forgiving to let go and detach themselves from the wrongdoer. When you choose to forgive, you release yourself from negative emotions like anger and bitterness and free yourself from being tied to the person who hurt you. Forgiveness is not about the other person; it's about you. Holding onto unforgiveness keeps you linked to the person who wronged you, causing you to act in ways you despise.

To *forgive* means to stop feeling resentment towards the offender, to pardon, and to let go. From a biblical perspective, Jesus pardoned us from sin and wrongdoing by giving His life. When we confess our sins and seek forgiveness, we are cleansed and set free. Jesus also

WILT THOU BE MADE WHOLE?

taught us to forgive others as we would like to be forgiven. Letting go of grudges, even when it's difficult, is essential for experiencing love, peace, and joy.

It's important to focus on freeing yourself from negative emotions and living a life filled with love, peace, and joy instead of dwelling on past wrongs. The book of Job, in Job 21:23–25 (NLT), illustrates how one person can die in prosperity while another lives in bitter poverty. Holding on to wrongs and failing to forgive can lead to physical diseases such as cancer, diabetes, and high blood pressure.

The Bible provides examples of forgiveness, such as Stephen's forgiveness of those who stoned him to death, as well as Joseph's forgiveness of his brothers who sold him into slavery. Joseph was able to forgive his brothers and let go of bitterness and anger to fulfill his calling, understanding that he was part of a larger divine plan.

What situation is God asking you to let go of? Is it the person who molested you and acted like nothing happened? Is it the fact that you were raised with only one parent and feel like you missed out on something? Were you in a two-parent home, and there was so much chaos that you felt like you had to remove yourself from that situation, but until you could find the time, place, and financial ability to escape, you started harboring hatred and bitterness, also making vows out of your emotions that caused you to go down a dark path? Then you started to blame everyone but yourself. Whatever the situation you are in, let go and let God. God is the only one that can free you. He has given salvation through Jesus Christ, his Son.

> For God so loved the world that He gave
> His only begotten Son. (John 3:16)

He has been the perfect example of forgiveness. As Jesus was ridiculed, spit on, made a spectacle of, lied about, beaten, and compelled to bear His cross, He was nailed to the cross, and through all this, one of His last words was, "Father, forgive them for they know not what they do." One of the disciples asked Jesus how many times we forgive—do we forgive seven times? Jesus said no, seventy times seven in one day. Seven is the number of perfection; you should never stop forgiving.

Forgiving is not easy when it seems as if the pain is so deep. Ask God to help you to forgive and keep forgiving until you know within yourself that there is nothing left. Think of it as if you had a sore, and until it is healed, you feel the pain, but when it is healed, there is no more pain. You might have a scar to remind you that something took place, but because of the healing, you can look at that scar and feel no pain. That's how it is with forgiveness; there is a scar, but it is just to remind you of the ability to overcome and let it go.

The word of God teaches us that if we have anything against our brother, we are to leave our gift at the altar, go and make it right with our brother, and then come and offer our gift at the altar. Think about it. It is hard to go to someone and confess to them what you have done and ask for forgiveness, but you must face up to and own what you did. Too often, we want to go to God and forget that we have hurt or offended our brother or sister.

Let's do it the right way: Confess your faults to one another and feel the freedom of the love of God flowing through you. Don't get bogged down with pride, for pride comes before a fall. Humble yourself and let it go. To unlock the shackles and chains of wrongs done and hold them over someone, forgive, and let it go. The key is forgiveness.

There are steps you can take to forgiveness:

1. Pray and ask God to help you to completely let go of the trespasser and the trespass.
2. Be consistent; keep crying out until you know that the transgression is out of your heart.
3. Forgive others, but also forgive yourself. Many times, as we go before God and ask for forgiveness, he forgives us and remembers it no more. But when we don't forgive ourselves, it gives the enemy access to our lives. He keeps bringing up things that God has vindicated us from, which still promotes bondage. Let yourself go.

WILT THOU BE MADE WHOLE?

4. Praise and worship God for setting you free, for whom the Son sets free is free indeed.
5. Walk in that freedom as children of God.

When you acknowledge that forgiveness frees you and are willing to open the lock and feel the freedom it brings, then the Spirit of God can move freely in your life, and you can live a life of love, joy, and peace. Not as the world gives, but only as it comes from God through his Son, Jesus Christ. It is your choice. Choose to forgive and go free. Praise the Lord!

Continuing growth and maintaining wholeness

The journey from victim to victor is not a destination but an ongoing process. Even as you embrace your identity in Christ, change your narrative, and begin to help others, it's crucial to continue growing and maintain the wholeness you've found.

Here are some key strategies for continuing growth and maintaining wholeness:

1. Stay rooted in God's Word: regular Bible study and meditation on Scripture will continue to renew your mind and strengthen your new identity in Christ.
2. Maintain a strong prayer life: keep an open line of communication with God, sharing your struggles, victories, and everyday experiences with Him.
3. Stay connected to a supportive community: surround yourself with fellow believers who can encourage you, hold you accountable, and remind you of your identity in Christ when you forget.
4. Practice self-care: take care of your physical, emotional, and mental health. This includes getting enough rest, eating well, exercising, and engaging in activities that bring you joy.

5. Continue to process and heal: recognize that healing is often layered. Be open to addressing new areas of hurt or trauma as they surface.
6. Set healthy boundaries: learn to say no to things that compromise your wholeness and yes to things that support your growth.
7. Serve others: continuing to use your testimony and experiences to help others can reinforce your own healing and growth.
8. Embrace ongoing learning: attend workshops, read books, or seek counseling to continue developing tools for maintaining wholeness.
9. Practice gratitude: regularly thank God for His work in your life. This helps maintain a positive perspective and reinforces your victor mentality.
10. Be patient with yourself: remember that growth is not always linear. There may be setbacks or difficult days, but these don't negate your progress.

Maintaining wholeness also involves being prepared for potential triggers or challenges. Develop a plan for how you'll respond when faced with situations that might tempt you to fall back into old patterns of thinking or behavior.

Remember, your identity in Christ is not based on your performance or feelings. On days when you struggle, remind yourself of who God says you are. Your wholeness is ultimately found in Him, not in your ability to maintain perfect behavior or emotions.

As you continue to grow, you may find that God uses you in increasingly significant ways to bring healing and hope to others. Embrace these opportunities, but always remember to keep your own spiritual, emotional, and physical health a priority.

In conclusion, living in victory is about embracing your identity in Christ, changing your narrative from victim to victor, using your testimony to help others, and committing to ongoing growth and wholeness. It's a journey that requires persistence, faith, and a continual reliance on God's strength and love. As you walk this path,

WILT THOU BE MADE WHOLE?

remember the words of the Apostle Paul in Philippians 1:6: "Being confident of this, that he who began a good work in you will carry it on to completion until the day of Christ Jesus." God is faithful to complete the work of healing and transformation he has begun in you.

Conclusion

Final Words of Encouragement

Beloved, as you stand at this threshold between your past and your future, know that you are not alone. The journey you've embarked upon is both challenging and rewarding, filled with moments of struggle and triumph. But take heart, for the Lord Himself walks beside you every step of the way.

Remember the words of Isaiah 43:18–19: "Forget the former things; do not dwell on the past. See, I am doing a new thing! Now it springs up; do you not perceive it? I am making a way in the wilderness and streams in the wasteland." God is calling you out of your past, out of the wilderness of victimhood, and into a new land of promise and wholeness.

Your journey to break free from the victim spirit is not just about personal healing; it's about generational transformation. By choosing to confront your past, embrace healing, and step into the fullness of who God created you to be, you're not only changing your own life but also paving the way for future generations to walk in freedom.

There may be times when the old patterns try to reassert themselves when the familiar comfort of victimhood calls out to you. In these moments, stand firm in the truth you now know. You are not defined by your past hurts or generational curses. You are defined by your identity in Christ—beloved, redeemed, and made whole.

Remember, healing is not a destination but a journey. There will be ups and downs, victories and setbacks. But with each step forward, you're growing stronger, more resilient, and more aligned with God's vision for your life. Celebrate every victory, no matter how small it may seem. Each one is a testament to the transformative power of God's love and your commitment to wholeness.

As you continue on this path, stay connected to your support system. Surround yourself with those who encourage your growth and affirm your journey. Keep engaging in the spiritual disciplines we've discussed—prayer, Scripture study, worship—for these are the lifelines that will sustain you in times of challenge.

Above all, hold fast to the truth that you are deeply loved by a God who sees you, knows you, and desires your wholeness. He is the ultimate source of your healing and the anchor for your soul. As Jeremiah 29:11 reminds us, "'For I know the plans I have for you,' declares the Lord, 'plans to prosper you and not to harm you, plans to give you hope and a future.'"

Call to action

Now, dear reader, it's time to take the next step. The knowledge you've gained and the insights you've uncovered are powerful, but they can only transform your life if put into action. Here's what I encourage you to do:

1. Make a declaration: Write out a personal declaration of freedom from the victim's spirit. Speak it aloud daily, affirming your identity in Christ and your commitment to wholeness.
2. Identify your next step: Based on what you've learned, what's the next practical step in your healing journey? Whether it's seeking counseling, joining a support group, or confronting a past hurt, commit to taking that step within the next week.
3. Start a healing journal: Begin documenting your journey. Record your struggles, victories, prayers, and the ways you see God working in your life. This will serve as a powerful reminder of your progress and God's faithfulness.

WILT THOU BE MADE WHOLE?

4. Practice forgiveness: Identify someone you need to forgive—including yourself. Begin the process of forgiveness, remembering that it's a journey, not a one-time event.

5. Share your story: Find a trusted friend or family member and share part of your story with them. Bringing your experiences into the light can be incredibly healing and may inspire others to seek wholeness as well.

6. Engage in community: Seek out a community of believers who can support you in your journey. This might be a small group at your church, a Bible study, or a recovery group.

7. Set boundaries: Identify areas in your life where you need to establish healthy boundaries. Begin implementing these boundaries, even if it feels uncomfortable at first.

8. Serve others: Look for opportunities to use your experiences to help others. This might be through formal ministry or simply by being available to listen and encourage someone who's struggling.

9. Cultivate gratitude: Start a daily gratitude practice. Each day, write down three things you're thankful for. This will help shift your focus from what's wrong to what's right in your life.

10. Commit to ongoing growth: Recognize that healing and growth are lifelong processes. Commit to continuing your journey of personal and spiritual development beyond the pages of this book.

Remember, the question "Wilt thou be made whole?" is not just a one-time inquiry. It's a daily invitation from Jesus to step into the fullness of life He offers. Each day, you have the opportunity to say "yes" to wholeness, to choose healing over hurt, freedom over bondage, and victory over victimhood.

As you close this book and step into the next chapter of your life, know that you carry with you the tools, insights, and, most importantly, the presence of God to break free from the victim spirit once and for all. You are no longer bound by your past or by generational curses. You are a new creation in Christ, empowered to live in freedom and to extend that freedom to others.

May you walk forward with confidence, knowing that the God who began this good work in you will carry it on to completion (Philippians 1:6). May you experience the depth of His love, the power of His healing, and the joy of living as a whole and victorious child of God.

The journey to wholeness is before you. Embrace it with courage, perseverance, and hope. You are made for more, and your best days are yet to come. Go forth and live in the fullness of all that God has for you. The victim spirit no longer has a hold on you. You are free indeed.

In the powerful and healing name of Jesus, Amen.

Prayer for healing and wholeness

We want to share a beautiful prayer for healing and wholeness to support your journey, and please feel free to read aloud:

Heavenly Father, I come before you in the name of Jesus Christ, thanking you for guiding me to this place of healing and wholeness. I am grateful for your daily protection and for the gift of salvation that has restored my connection with You as the author and perfecter of my faith.

I am blessed by the path you have laid for me to walk in holiness every day and for the peaceful and blessed life, you have allowed me to live. I declare that Your people will submit themselves to you, and I ask for the revelation of our hearts, knowing that only You can understand my innermost thoughts and desires. Help me to forgive those who have hurt or wronged me and cleanse my heart of any unforgiveness.

Deliver me from anything that seeks to harm me, whether external forces or my self-destructive tendencies. Grant me a selfless heart that looks out for the needs of others. Father, I pray for the salvation of souls and the healing of sickness and disease among Your people, believing in miracles, signs, and wonders.

Help me to cast away fear and anxiety, knowing that I can trust You with all my cares. Despite the challenges of this world, I find assurance in You, knowing that all is well because my confidence rests in You. I trust you with my life and thank You for making me whole in Christ Jesus. In Jesus's name, Amen.

About the Authors

Dr. Brenda Howard has served as the senior pastor and overseer at Tabernacle of Prayer Christian Fellowship in Macon, Georgia, for twenty-eight years. In 2007, Dr. Howard earned her doctor of ministry in Christian counseling. She is also the author of two books and has conducted ministry work in various countries, including the Republic of Panama, England, Africa, Switzerland, and Germany.

Dr. C. B. Howard is a highly regarded professional with three decades of experience in higher education. Dr. Howard is known for his extensive expertise and collaborative leadership, which have led to significant contributions in the field of higher education. Dr. Howard's educational background includes a bachelor's degree in psychology, a master's in education in educational administration, a doctorate in education in educational leadership and management, and a doctorate in ministry in Christian counseling.

www.ingramcontent.com/pod-product-compliance
Lightning Source LLC
Chambersburg PA
CBHW030040201224
19271CB00045B/782